ENCORE WITH RECTANGLE AND PHILOSOPHY

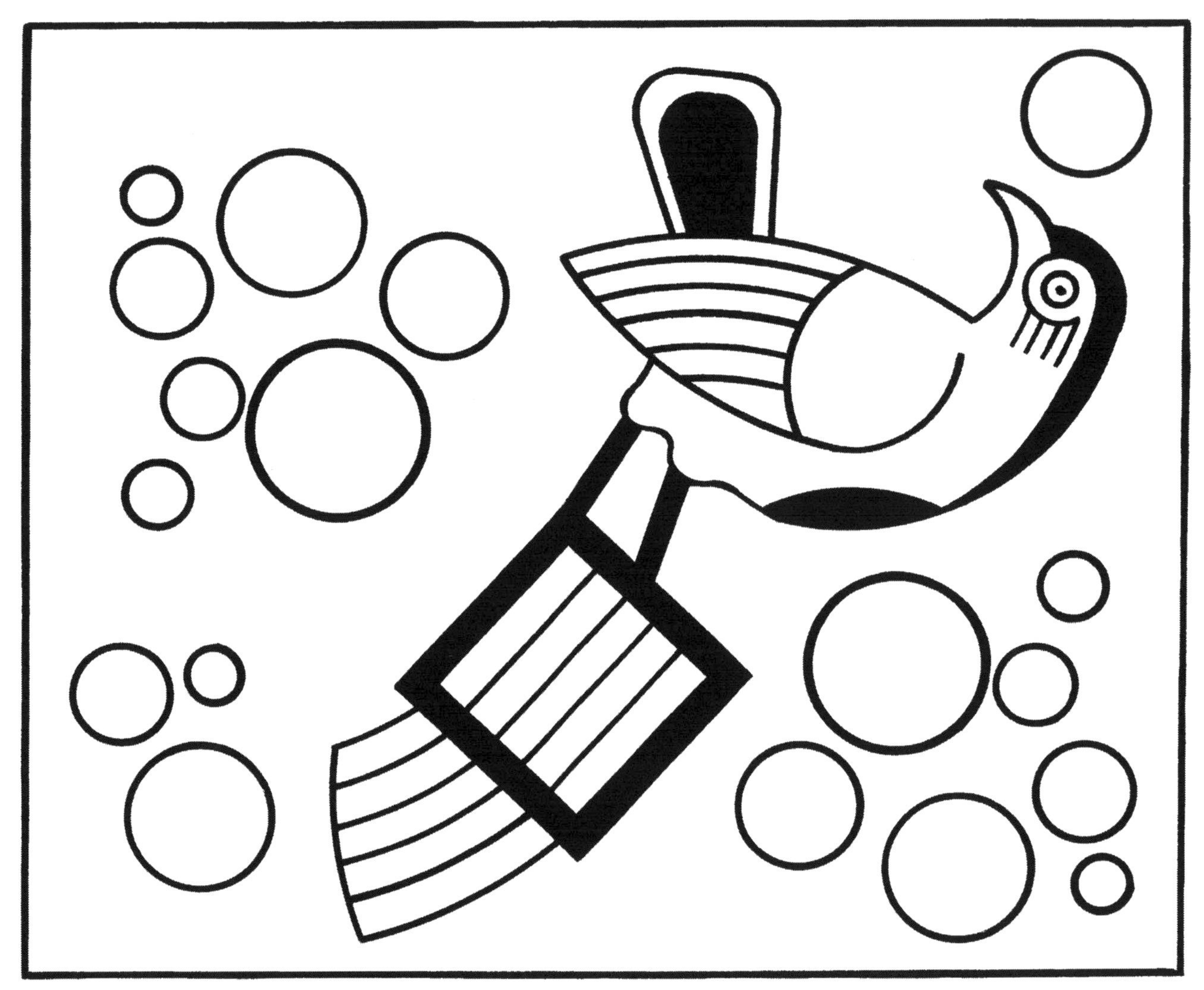

ENCORE WITH RECTANGLE AND PHILOSOPHY

Ron Padgett & Trevor Winkfield

CUNEIFORM PRESS

Encore with Rectangle and Philosophy

> *I built a house*
> *and had ideas in it.*
> —Ron Padgett

Initio it was weird,

everything,

Boom!

ribbons and shimmering everywhere,

and this and thisness:

stop, look, and sound too

waiting to come out

as soon as movement said to,

and a bone walked around

as if something had happened to it,

like, an infinity ago.

•

Excuse me.

I have to get up

and walk around a little.

My abode

is dark and cozy

but sometimes it turns me

into a bowling ball,

and yes

I weigh sixteen pounds

and am suddenly marbleized

as I hook into the pocket

and decimate all ten pins

in one explosive explosion!

—Wait, *decimate*

is not the *mot juste*,

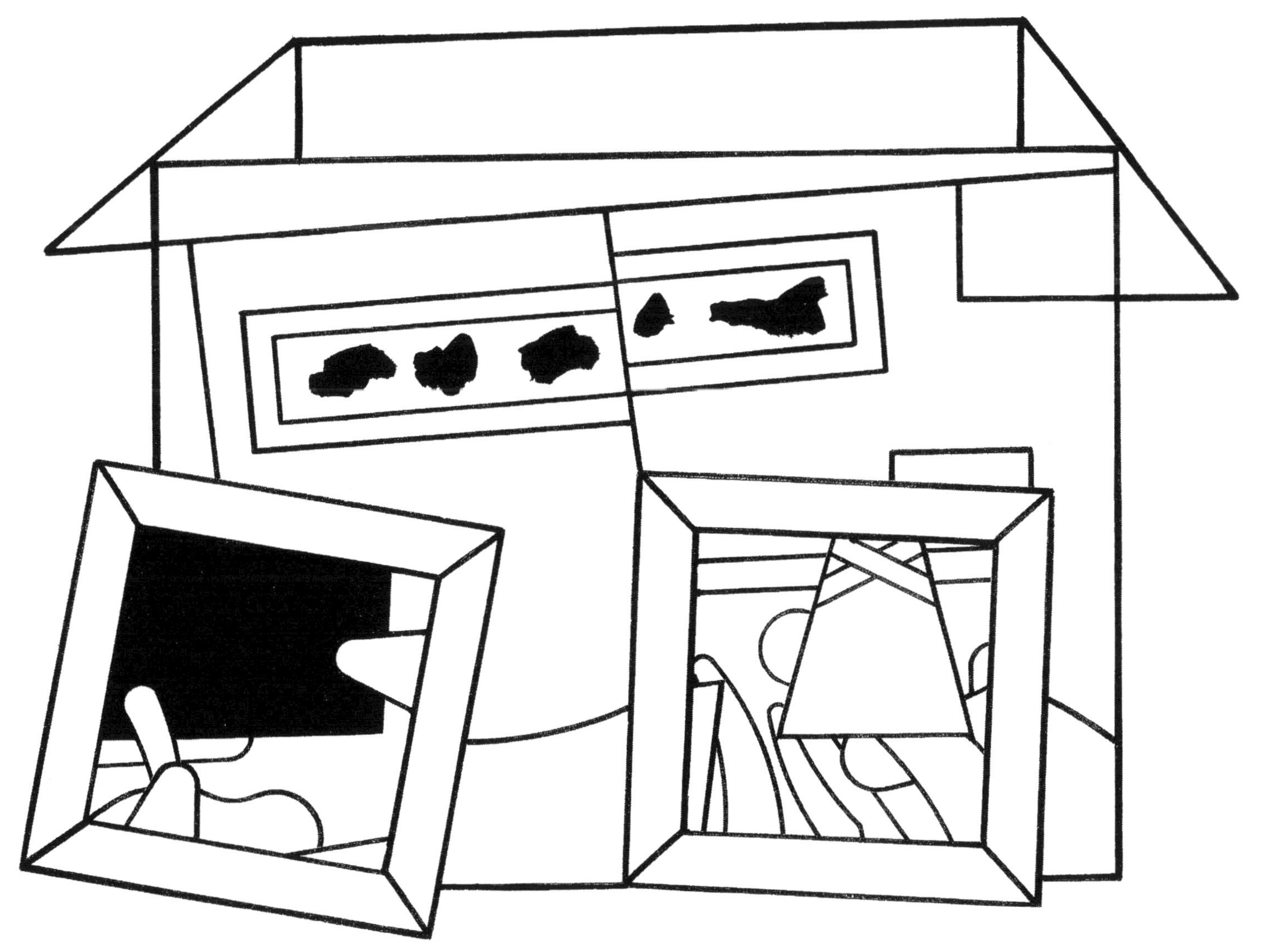

nor *cave* nor *bowling ball.*

(My soul has just multiplied itself,

in case.)

On second thought,

I don't think

I *can* get up.

Would you give me a hand?

Shakespeare?

What is Shakespeare?

The fellow bound

upon a wheel of fire

and rolled up into the sky?

•

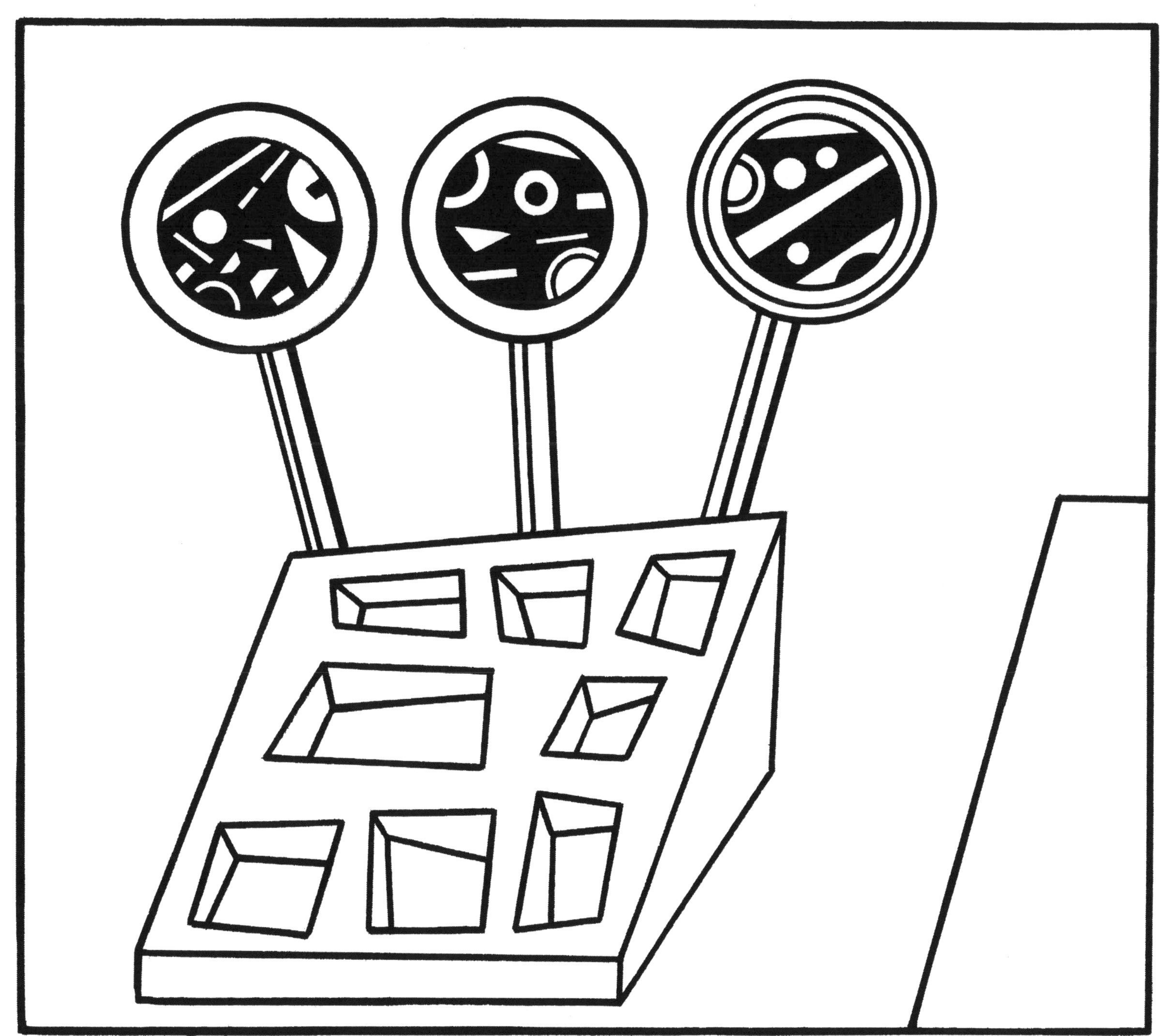

I'm stuck to a moment,

then it goes away.

I am not stuck to the world,

I *am* the world,

two feet tall

and zero deep and wide.

Look at the picture

in the dictionary

next to the word *mysticism*:

there's nothing there.

What do you think about

that?

(You're coming out of the wrong side of my head.)

•

Pronouns aren't for everybody.

•

My head went into everybody

the way vowels went into words

and life was a little easier,

then,

the way the Pacific Ocean

was easier than the Atlantic

and *best* was better than *better*,

and the barnyard swung open

in a kind of orchestral majesty

that got sucked into a pile of cow dung,

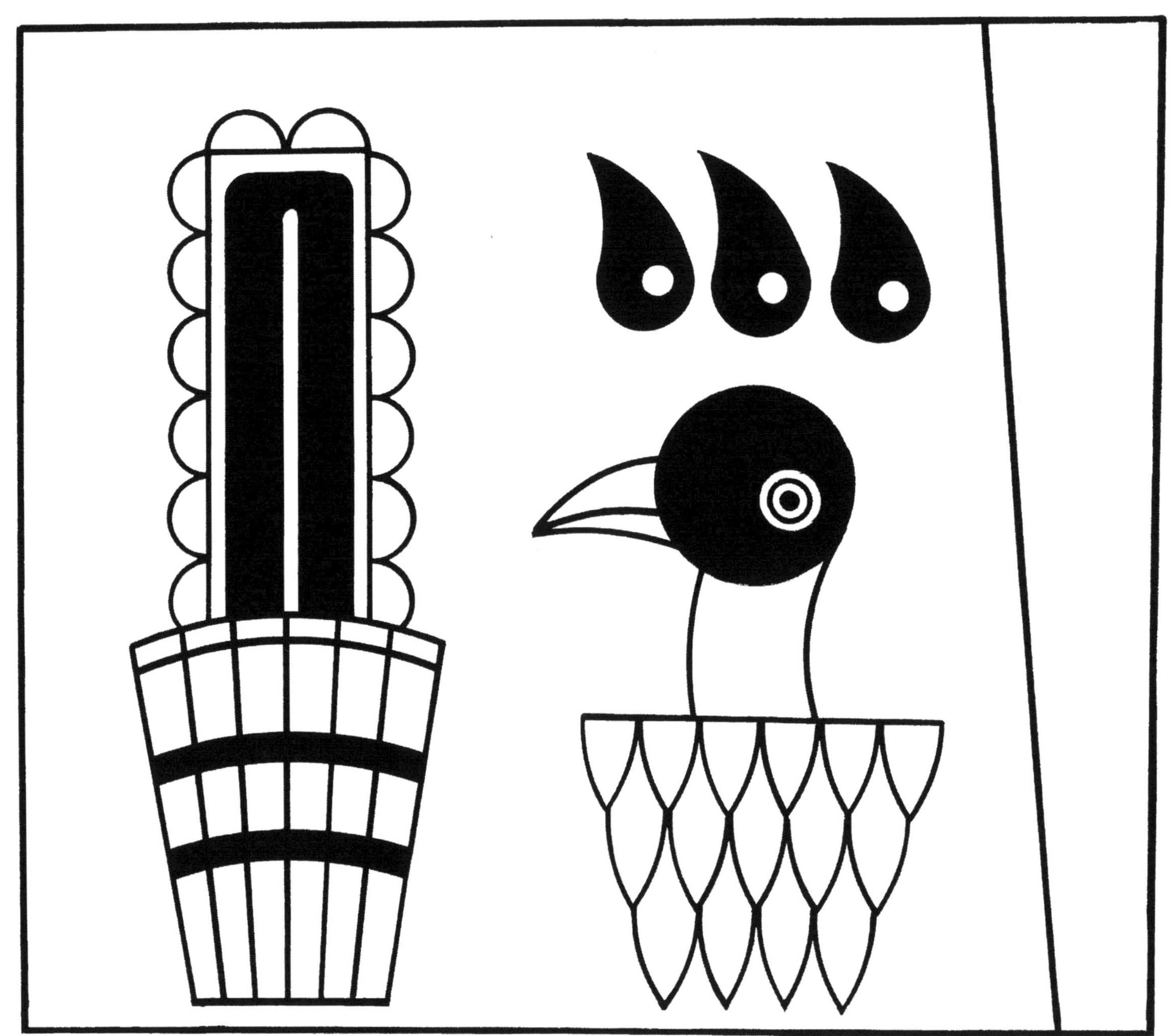

which caused ancient China to wake up

and be modern China, smiling

and gesturing Oh hello! and everything.

I gave the driver some yuan

and got out of the taxi, inwardly,

and then got out outwardly,

the driver went forward

into a pile of cow dung.

I figured there was time,

but for what?

Everybody went into my head

when harmony went into music.

●

There are a lot of details in the world

—too many for me, so

I *blur* them, using my ability to *blur*,

except now instead of you

I see invisible ink and it's thrilling

in a different way (for me,

not for you).

•

In the middle

of the night

What

is the name of that island

we went to

way back when and what

should be done with my ashes?

It had two pronunciations,

one for its citizens, one

for the rest of us. Released

into the stream in Vermont, perhaps.

Aside from The Hague,

how many cities begin (in English)

with The?

●

Antigua.

I wrote it down.

●

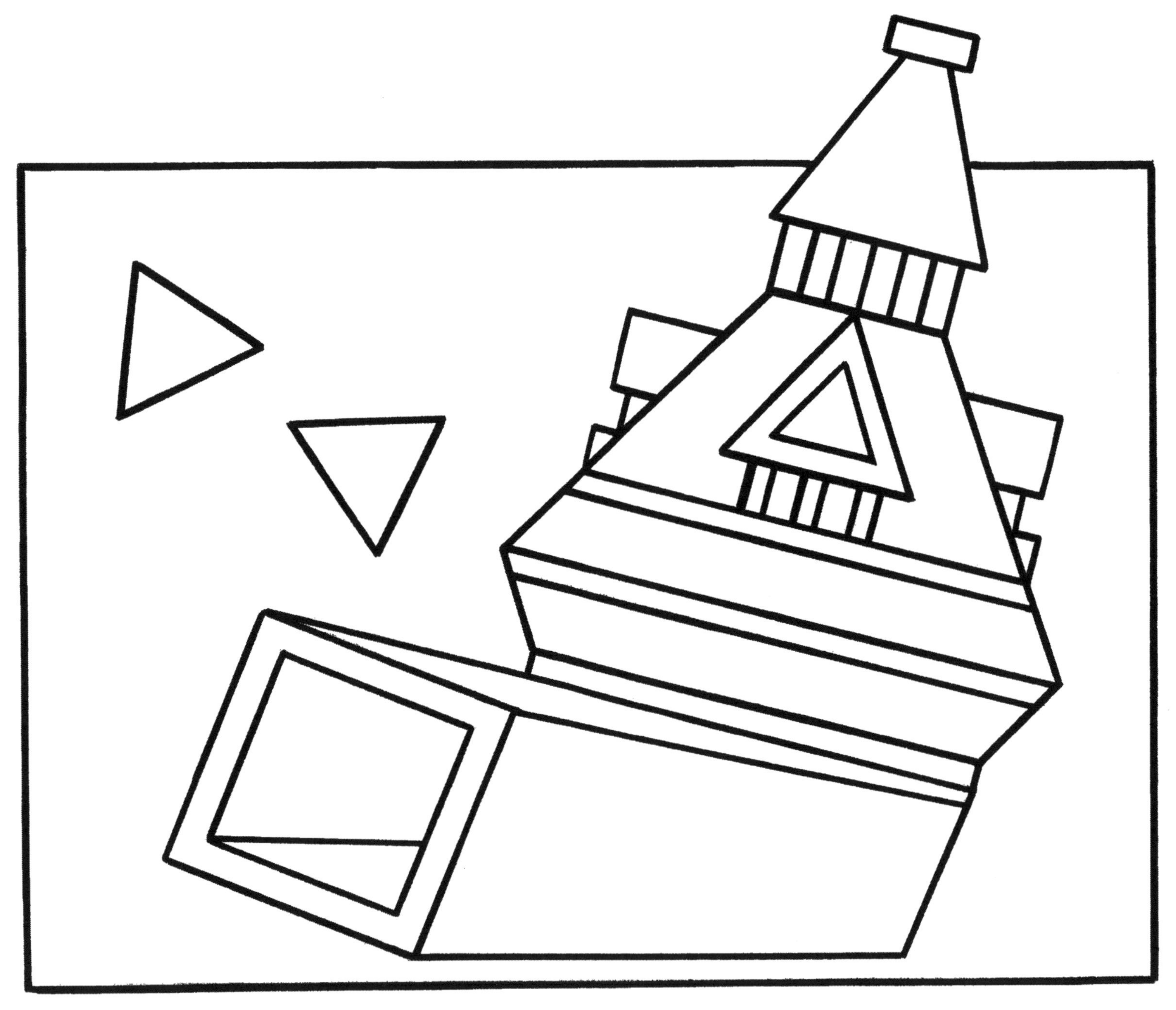

If you think

about the tasks

ahead of you

in the day,

go ahead and turn them

into small rectangles,

sweep them

into your hand

and toss them outside.

Then kill yourself.

●

The Bronx.

I wrote it up.

●

Beating so.

You give your hand to me

and then you say hello,

but I can hardly speak

my heart is...

...like the fork *now*

falling toward the floor and everything

falling as you grab grab grab

•

O my.

That's what people used to say.

God had left the sentence.

O me.

●

Coleridge

sat alone under a lime tree,

missing his friends,

and wrote about it—

a bird flew past,

electrifying,

the first time that something happened

during the writing of a poem

and got included.

Okay, first a bat goes by

and then a bee is singing,

and then the bird (a rook)

"(Now a dim speck, now vanishing in light)."

The bat and the bee I forgot

but that bird is bang on.

•

The idea of ⅓

is more appealing

than the idea of ⅔.

•

I built a house

that had ideas in it.

Am I supposed to be

the something of something?

•

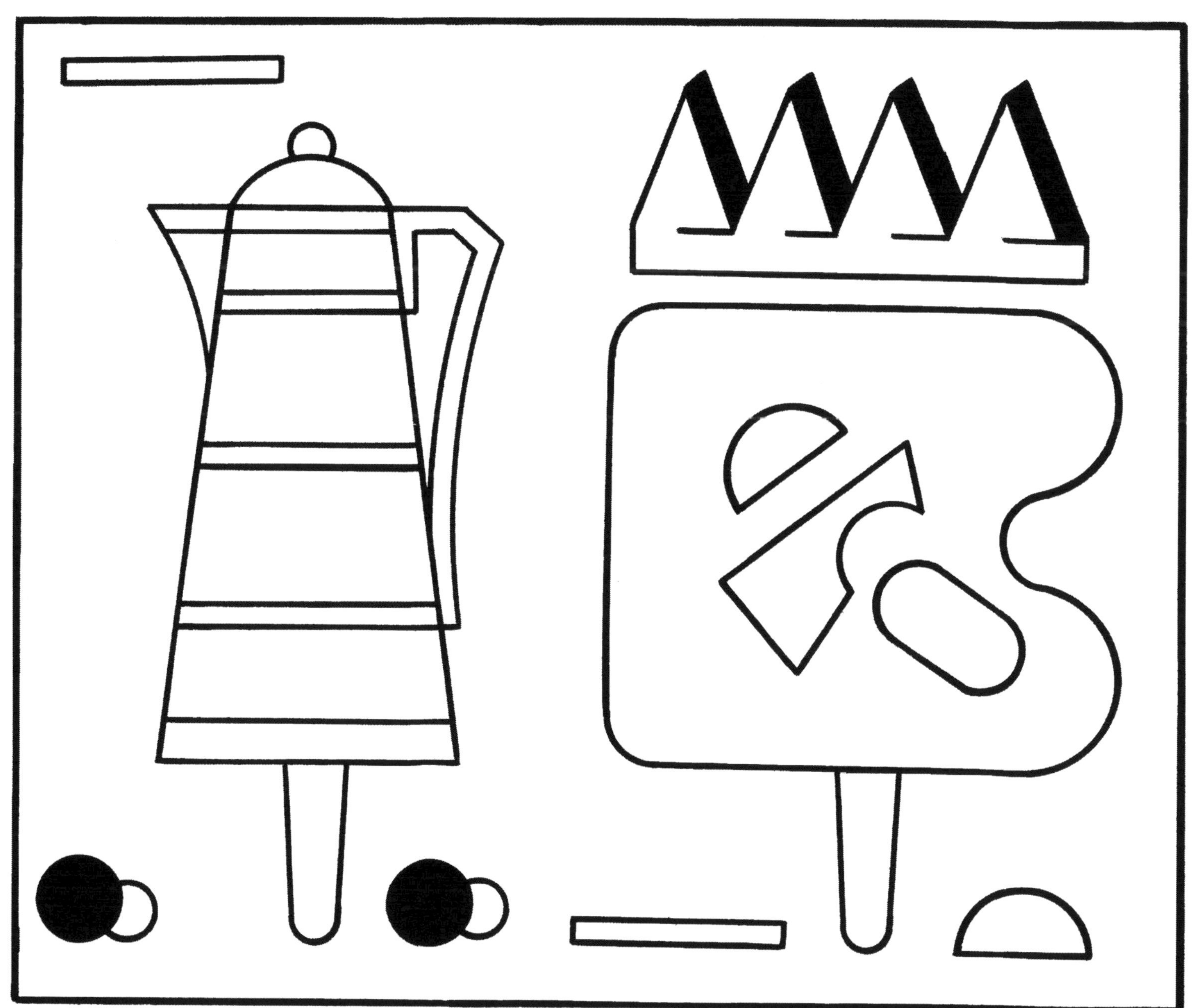

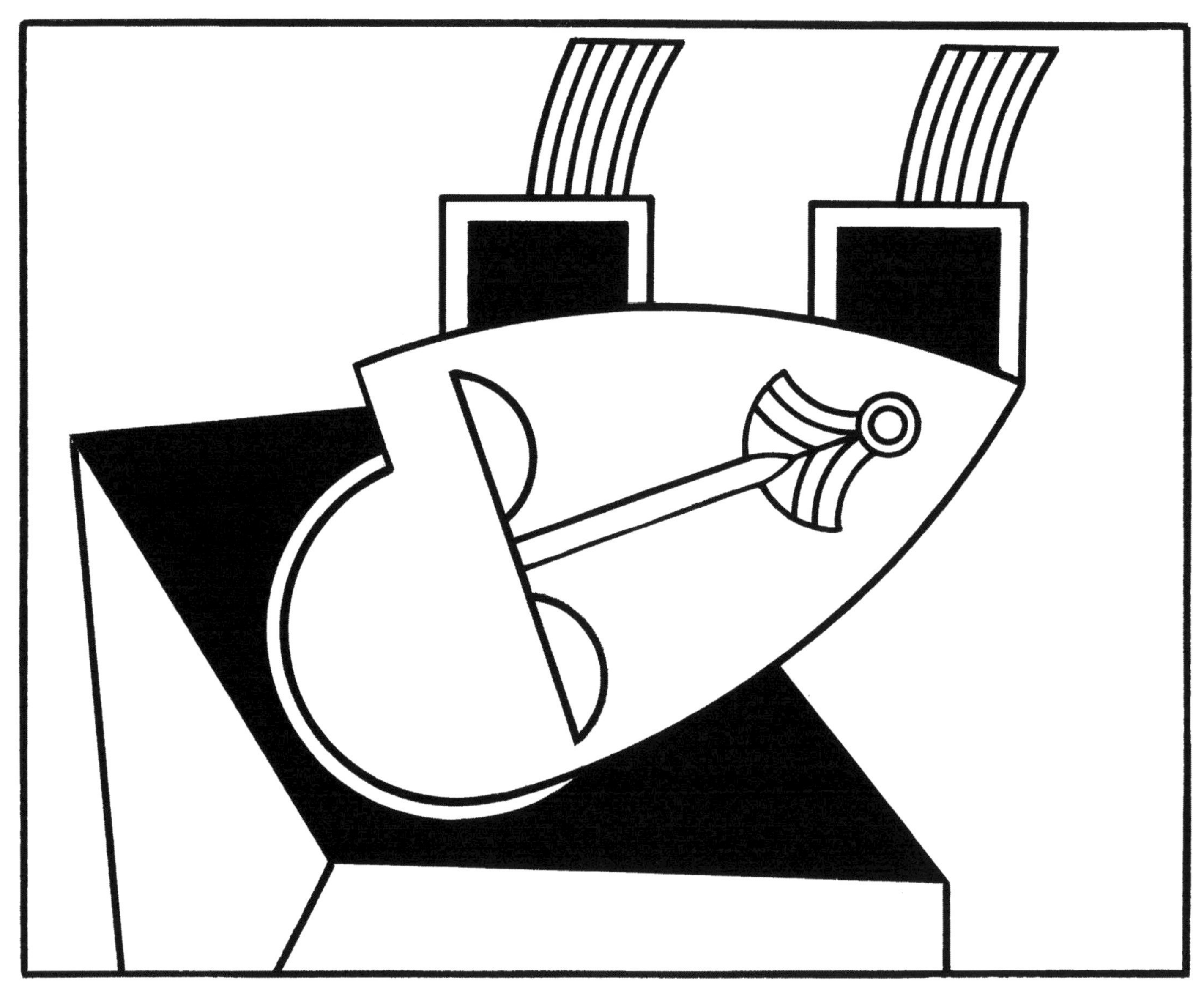

It's a long way

between love of country

and licking your lips.

You're told to love your country

by people who want you

to obey them but never tell you

that you should lick your lips

before trying to eat or drink something

that might burn them.

●

Don't "go" "there."

(Or the bell will ring.)

•

I dreamed there was

an athletic team called

The Tokyo Infinities.

How could there be

more than one infinity?

Like, say, seventeen of them.

Maybe each member

has his own infinity.

Their uniforms were orange and black.

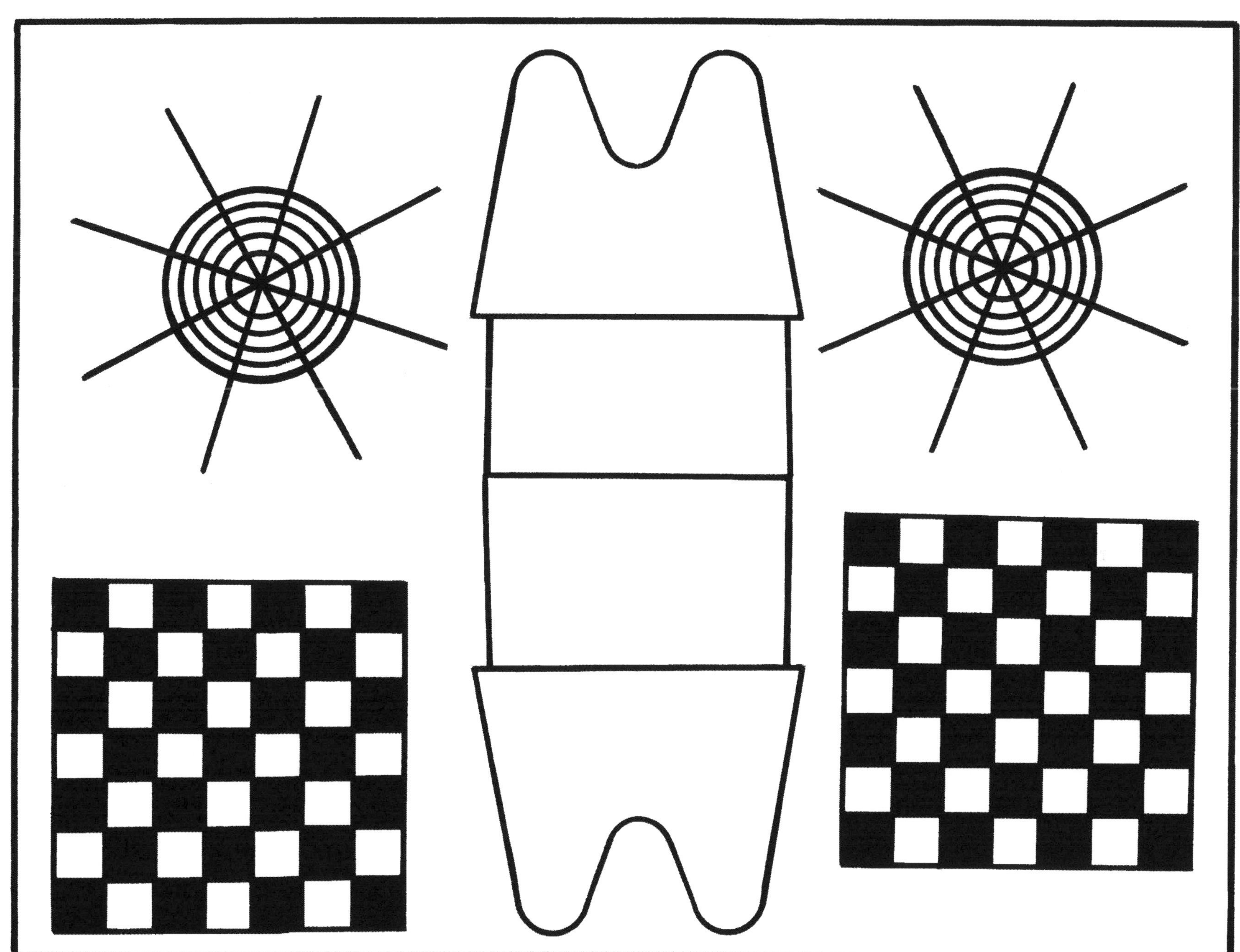

•

When Coleridge says "now" in his poem

he means now, whenever that was or is:

Now—a dim concept,

vanished in light

that vanished in the dark.

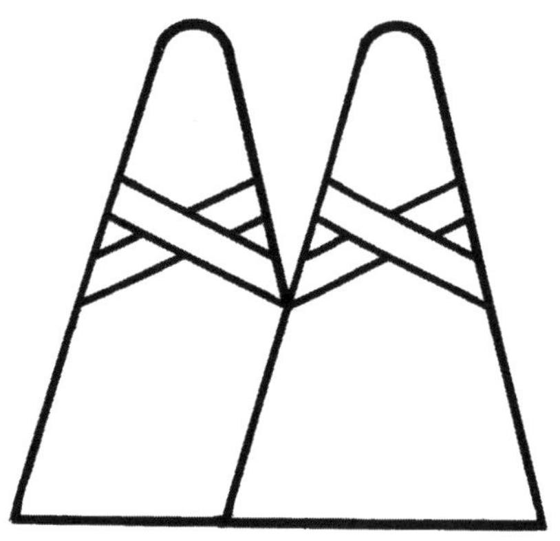

Encore with Rectangle and Philosophy was printed in
an edition of five hundred copies, of which twenty-six
are lettered and signed by the author and artist.

Published by:
Cuneiform Press
www.cuneiformpress.com

ISBN: 978-1-950055-02-9
Text © 2019 by Ron Padgett
Art © 2019 by Trevor Winkfield

Distributed by:
Small Press Distribution
www.spdbooks.org